MEERKATS

THE WILDLIFE COLLECTION

Contents

4

8

26

46

Introduction 4

Evolution 8

Species 14

Habitat 18

Vocalization and Communication 22

Diet and Foraging 26

Anatomy 30

Reproduction and Young 34

Behavior 40

Population 46

Long-term Survival 48

Conservation and Popular Culture 56

First published in the UK in 2014

This edition published by Park Lane Books

www.parklanebooks.com

Printed in China

ISBN: 978-1-906969-81-3

Designed by: BrainWave

Creative Director: Kevin Gardner

Written by: Lisa Hughes

Images courtesy of PA Photos, Corbis and Shutterstock

Introduction

Meerkats, also known as suricates, are small mammals belonging to the mongoose family. These highly social creatures have long been a source of fascination, displaying altruistic tendencies in their tight-knit communities. Unlike their nocturnal relations, meerkats are diurnal creatures and will only leave the safety of their burrows during daylight hours.

Wild meerkats are exclusive to southern African areas. They can be found in South Africa, the Namib Desert in Namibia, and the Kalahari Desert in Botswana and have adapted to suit desert life. These sociable creatures live in large communities in a network of underground burrows and work together to protect the group from predators. A meerkat community is called a mob, gang, or clan. Typical clans consist of a dominant breeding pair and their offspring of several litters usually totaling approximately 20 meerkats, although some supersize families are home to up to 50. These large meerkat families enable them to work harmoniously together. Babysitting, excavating and maintaining their complex burrow systems, mentoring young, and sentry duties are all part of meerkat life irrespective of their gender. The role of the sentry is vital. They will act as the lookouts for predators and warn the clan of any danger, with their unique bark or whistle. Meerkats are agile climbers and will scale a tree or bush in order to find the best vantage point. The African plains are home to several birds of prey including hawks and eagles – both of which will hunt meerkats – so having a few members of the clan keeping a watchful eye out enables the rest of the group to forage for food. Foraging for food is a vital daily requirement, as meerkats have no excess body fat and can lose up to five per cent of their body weight during the night.

Being omnivores, the meerkat diet is varied. They primarily eat insects but will also eat lizards, small mammals, eggs, and fruit should such a meal present itself. They have adapted wonderfully to the arid environment of the Kalahari and Namib deserts and can survive on very little water. In fact they are able to get their daily water requirement from their diet, which is a contributing factor as to why they are able to flourish in such dry conditions. Meerkats forage as part of a group but will catch and kill their own prey. Much of the meerkat's way of life is learned behavior as opposed to instinct. As pups and juveniles they will watch and learn from their elders all manner of skills including foraging, catching and killing difficult prey items, communication, and fighting. They are even taught about some of their predators, such as snakes, through mobbing an unwelcome guest in their territory. Mobbing is also used to deter a threat to the clan. The behavior they display involves grouping together to appear more intimidating. They will surround a snake while

■ **ABOVE:** **A pair of meerkat sentinels looking at their surroundings in the Kalahari Desert in Africa.**

- **ABOVE: A group of meerkats on full alert for danger.**
- **OPPOSITE: On lookout duty in the Kalahari Desert in Botswana.**
- **BELOW: Three-week-old meerkat pups at Bristol Zoo Gardens, England.**

making threatening spit calls, occasionally lashing out to poke and scratch at it. These actions are only possible when the clan moves together as a group, as an individual meerkat would not be a match for a hungry and venomous predator looking for a quick meal.

Although they are classed as "least concern" by the International Union for the Conservation of Nature (IUCN), meerkats are an important part of desert life and need to be preserved in their natural habitat. Research projects have been formed in order for us to better understand the evolution of their co-operative behavior and social structure, with the most notable project to date being the Kalahari Meerkat Project. This long-term research facility has contributed to a number of meerkat specific wildlife programs, including the worldwide popular show *Meerkat Manor*, which was aired for four seasons on Animal Planet between 2005 and 2008.

Since meerkats were first introduced to the general public through wildlife documentaries in the 1980s, they have continued to grow in popularity around the world. Many zoological and wildlife centers are home to captive meerkats, which are always popular with visitors. This, teamed with heartwarming TV shows and movies, has led to these comical and intriguing creatures becoming one of the world's favorite animals.

Evolution

■ **ABOVE: Meerkats have evolved over 60 million years.**

Binomial Name: Suricata suricatta
Class: Mammalia
Order: Carnivora
Suborder: Feliformia
Family: Herpestidae

Suricata suricatta is the scientific name for suricates, better known as meerkats. It is thought that the name meerkat comes from early Dutch settlers in the region that described the nimble creatures to be "meer kat dan hond," which translates to "more cat than dog." Another theory is that the name is descendant from the Afrikaans word "meercatte" and roughly translates as "marsh cat" or "lake cat." The meerkat has also been named the "sun angel" in the Zimbabwean region, as according to folklore it protects villages from the moon devil.

The evolution of meercats can be traced back to the demise of the dinosaurs by looking at their family and order. Meerkats belong to the suborder Feliformia (sometimes know as Feloidea), which consists of "cat-like" carnivorous species

■ **ABOVE: Banded mongooses on the alert in the Masai Mara Game Reserve, Kenya.**

including cats, hyenas, mongooses, and civets.

There are seven extant families in the Feliformia suborder which include Felidae (cats, tigers, lions), Eupleridae (carnivorans restricted to the island of Madagascar), Hyaenidae (hyenas, aardwolf), Herpestidae (mongooses, meerkats), Nandiniidae (single species of African palm civet), Prionodontidae (Asiatic linsangs), and Viverridae (civets, genets, African linsangs).

Meerkats belong to the Herpestidae family, but until 1993 they were placed in the Viverridae family before it was discovered that herpestids are genetically different from viverrids. Although Feliformia species are a suborder of the Carnivora, several herpestid species are omnivores and will include fruit and tubers in their diet.

Evolution can be traced back 60 million years to the Paleogene Period, which follows the downfall of non-avian dinosaurs, when Miacoidea appears. This superfamily was divided into two carnivorous families: Miacidae and Viverravidae. The miacids were of similar size to mongoose species today and are thought to have survived on a diet of insects and small mammals. Approximately 42 million years ago, the miacids branched into two distinct groups: the Caniforms and the Feliforms. Unfortunately, there are considerable gaps in fossil records, which make it impossible to know the clear Feliform families and their evolutionary path.

■ **ABOVE: Always alert, a family of meerkats.**

Meerkats are believed to have evolved from the suricata suricatta major, a type of extinct meerkat that was found at the southern tip of Africa. The extinct meerkat was a close relation and shared many similarities to the banded mongoose, which can still be seen today. It is thought that as the climate became drier, meerkats evolved to survive in the desert-like environment.

Suricata suricatta major shared many anatomical similarities to their mongoose relations; they were of a similar size and weight to the banded mongoose, and both shared features such as muscular limbs, small ears, strong claws, and a long tail. The subspecies suricata suricatta major no longer exists today due to evolutionary development but many similarities can still be seen between meerkats and the banded mongoose.

The banded mongoose shares a similar diet feeding on insects, millipedes, small reptiles, and birds. Unlike meerkats, the banded mongoose does not do well in desert conditions and favors open forests and grassland with access to water. However, they do share the same tight-knit community living arrangements as their meerkat relations.

Meerkats have undergone a series of changes that enable them to survive in the drier regions of southern Africa. Their coat color has changed to suit the sandy terrain, and they have darker bands of fur surrounding their eyes. This feature acts like built-in "sunglasses," which enable them to search the sky for predators.

Meerkats can run on all four legs at a top speed of approximately 20mph. They can also stand on their hind legs with the aid of their long tail; this provides them with a better vantage point when on sentry duty.

Life in the desert would be incredibly difficult for a single meerkat and they are heavily dependent on their social structure. Group living increases their chances of survival, especially when there are so many aerial and terrestrial predators that would welcome a meerkat as a meal. Evolution of the meerkat's social structure includes mobbing behavior. Mobbing is a technique used to drive away a threat or predator. The meerkats line up or surround a threat and will lash out by biting, poking, and making intimidating spit calls. As individuals they would stand very little chance against a predator, such as the cape cobra, but by working together, the risk to each individual is reduced. It is also believed that this mobbing behavior is used as a way for the young to learn about different predators.

■ **ABOVE: Safety in numbers in the Kalahari Desert, South Africa.**

■ **ABOVE LEFT: A meerkat sticking its head out of its burrow, showing off the dark bands of fur surrounding its eyes, Botswana.**

■ **LEFT: A meerkat family running across the salt pan, Makgadikgadi Pans, Kalahari Desert, Botswana.**

Species

■ ABOVE: **Slender-tailed meerkats in the Kalahari Gemsbok National Park, South Africa.**

It is thought that there are 12 subspecies of meerkat, although to date only three of these have been confirmed. These are:

Suricata suricatta siricata
Suricata suricatta majoriae
Suricata suricatta iona

The suricata suricatta siricata was discovered in 1776 and is the most well-known subspecies usually found in South Africa, Botswana, and in all parts of the Kalahari Desert. They are often referred to as the slender-tailed meerkat. Their coat colors vary between shades of orange and brown, the perfect camouflage for the bright colored sand found in the Kalahari region. Many meerkat documentaries are based on this particular subspecies. They are also the most common type of meerkats that are found in captivity.

Suricata suricatta majoriae was discovered in 1936. They have a paler coat color and have distinctive bands around the eyes. Their coat coloring and facial features enable them to survive in the Namib Desert, which has lighter sand than the Kalahari Desert. They are slightly sturdier and have a larger head and chest. This subspecies is rarely seen in captivity. The

2010 National Geographic wildlife documentary *Clan of the Meerkat* was filmed in the Namib Desert and is based on a clan of the majoriae subspecies.

Suricata suricatta iona is native to Angola and was discovered in 1971. There is little information about the iona subspecies, as they are only found in a small part of southwestern Angola in the Iona National Park. It is thought that there may be another nine subspecies of meerkat, however until further research and studies of these possible subspecies have been carried out, there is no certainty of their confirmation.

The suspected subspecies include:

Suricata suricatta hahni

Suricata suricatta capensis

Suricata suricatta zenik

Suricata suricatta namaquensis

Suricata suricatta tertradactyl

Suricata suricatta vivierrina

Suricata suricatta typicus

Suricata suricatta hamiltoni

Suricata suricatta lophurous

■ **OPPOSITE: Sitting upright in the Namib Desert.**

■ **RIGHT: Whatever the species or subspecies, they are always on the lookout.**

Habitat

■ **ABOVE: A meerkat family standing guard in the Kalahari Desert, Botswana.**

■ **BELOW: A group of meerkats shelter in their burrow.**

Meerkats are found exclusively in southern parts of Africa in the dry desert-like areas of Botswana, South Africa, Angola, and Namibia. Meerkats are native to both the Namib Desert and the Kalahari Desert.

The Namib Desert extends across the Angolan and Namibian borders and stretches for more than 1,300 miles along the western coast of Africa. Statistically, it is the driest desert in Africa and is the only "true" desert in the southern part of the continent. With an annual precipitation of only two-20mm, the Namib is a harsh and unforgiving environment that supports very few species of animal. Arthropods are by far the most common, and only a few small animals have developed techniques to survive the harsh conditions. To the southeast, the Namib merges with the Kalahari Desert.

The Kalahari Desert dominates much of the region, covering Botswana and parts of South Africa and Namib. It extends to 600,000 square miles with the surrounding Kalahari Basin covering more than 1.6 million square miles. The Kalahari supports many more flora and fauna than a true desert, such as the Namib Desert to the west, and meerkats have adapted remarkably to thrive in the arid plains of this semi-desert. The summer temperatures in the Kalahari are very high, soaring to around 115°F (40°C). Sand temperatures can reach over 158°F (70°C).

■ **ABOVE: An African ground squirrel in Botswana.**

Between May and September are the winter months with highs of 70°F (22°C) and lows of 14°F (-10°C) during the cold desert nights. As diurnal mammals, meerkats venture from the safety of the burrows during daylight hours. They are most active early in the morning and early evening while the temperature isn't too hot. During the hottest part of the day they retreat back to the burrows to cool down.

The average rainfall is low, with a mere 12 inches (300 millimeters) during the latter end of the summer months. During these months the landscape is transformed with lush vegetation covering the plains, and ancient dry riverbeds called omuramba become standing pools of water. The Okavango River is the only permanent river in the region, which flows into an endorheic basin called the Okavango Delta in the northwest of the Kalahari Desert. This swamp-like area supports a vast array of flora and fauna and is known as the jewel of the Kalahari. The limited water source in the region has led meerkats to naturally evolve and develop, enabling them to get their required daily fluid intake from the food that they eat. They have a 40 per cent lower metabolic rate than other small mammals from other parts of the world, enabling them to survive with less food and water.

The Kalahari Desert terrain is made up of both soft and compacted sands, which can be found in various shades of red, orange, and white. The loose soft sand is favored when foraging for food, as the meerkats are able to move vast amounts of sand in a matter of seconds. When choosing a burrow site, the more compact sand is preferred. They usually live in burrows that have been dug by other small animals and will add to the network of tunnels to suit their needs, but can build their homes from scratch should the need call for it. The clan work together when creating or renovating their complex underground burrows and have also been known to share their dwelling with African ground squirrels and the yellow mongoose. Their differing diets eliminate competition for food, enabling the mixed species to live harmoniously alongside one another. Dung beetles are also often found sharing the residence and come in useful for cleaning up after the meerkats. As meerkats don't eat these types of beetle, the insects are able to live without the worry that they are soon to become the mammals' next meal.

The meerkat burrow consists of entrances and exits, tunnels and chambers, and can span anywhere between one and three miles, depending on the size of the clan. They can

■ **ABOVE: A yellow mongoose with its young in Botswana.**

tunnel down as much as two meters below ground which makes the ideal chambers for sleeping in, as the temperature remains fairly consistent.

As the burrows cover such a vast area of land, it is essential that there are plenty of entrances and exits, with some supersize burrows having up to 70 openings at various points throughout the habitual area. Scattered around the meerkat territory are dozens of boltholes. These are specially designed tunnels that are able to hold a group of meerkats should they hear a sentry warning call for danger. These boltholes provide them with a safe hiding place when a predator is in the vicinity, and with so many boltholes within their territory, the meerkats memorize their locations so they are able to run to the closest opening when required.

Underground, within the network of tunnels, they have between six and 15 dens made up of several sleeping and breeding burrows. Meerkats often move to a new den every few days. The only exception is the breeding burrow where the offspring are born, which the meerkats will remain in for up to three weeks before moving to a new den within the burrow. The reason for this continual rotation is primarily for parasite control. As the build-up of ticks and fleas becomes apparent in the den, the meerkats will move. Meerkats will also urinate and defecate in their burrows as the threat of predators leaves them too vulnerable to venture out alone. Moving to a new den gives the resident dung beetles a chance to clean up after the meerkats, with the feces left behind becoming a meal for the insects.

Breeding burrows have higher mounds of sand at their entrances, the result of the endless renovation required to keep the tunnels and chambers accessible for a longer period of time. Excavating and renovating burrow systems is a joint effort and meerkats will work one behind the other to systematically shift the sand out of the way.

Meerkats will stay in the breeding burrow for approximately three weeks. This gives the pups the opportunity to leave the burrow and begin their lessons in foraging for food with the adults, before moving on to a new den. Meerkats tend to return to the same breeding burrow time after time. When pups are present, the yellow mongoose that often shares the burrow with the meerkats, is chased away. This is because they have been known to eat a meerkat pup.

Meerkats are fiercely territorial and an alpha male will mark their territory using their scent glands. As meerkat clans are usually quite large, their territory will overlap with a rival family, which can result in many disputes leading to the stronger clan pushing the weaker gang out of their burrow system and forcing them to seek a new home.

Meerkats sometimes choose to move to a new territory if food becomes scarce. On the whole, meerkat families stick together to ensure the long-term survival of their clan. This altruistic attitude is a contributing factor to how these remarkable creatures are able to flourish in such a harsh environment.

■ **ABOVE: Marking the territory by scent marking in the Kalahari Desert, Botswana.**

Vocalization and Communication

Meerkats use three distinct methods of communicating with one another for different purposes. They use scent, body language, and vocal communicative sounds.

Studies have shown that wild meerkats living in the Kalahari Desert are able to recognize clan members through vocal calls and sounds. Vocal communication of this level of sophistication is evident in primates and now, after researchers from the University of Zurich conducted a study in October 2011, their findings suggest that meerkats too can single out and communicate with individual clan members through the sound and timbre of their voice.

These incredible mammals also have 20 different sounds, each with different meanings. Meerkats can produce sounds that include grunts, barks, growls, chirrups, chattering, trills, clicks, and whistles. They also make a purring sound when they are relaxed and content. Their calls can be broken down into six main categories which include guarding calls, alarm calls, lost calls, leading the group calls, pup feeding/begging calls, and foraging calls.

Their alarm calls not only warn the clan of an intruder, but also actually change in sound and urgency according to

- **ABOVE: A meerkat sounding the alarm.**
- **BELOW: A stunning photograph of a family group on alert.**

the type of threat or predator in the vicinity. The acoustic characteristics of the alarm call can inform group members whether the predator is aerial or terrestrial and can also notify them whether it's of low, medium, or high urgency that they should run for cover. The clan respond according to which signal they hear. If they are warned of an aerial predator, such as a martial eagle, they will scan the skies to register the intruder or will crouch down quietly, using their coats as camouflage in order to blend in to the surrounding landscape and will minimize movement so that they go unnoticed. If the signal they receive from the sentry warns them of a terrestrial predator, such as a black-backed jackal, the meerkats will seek shelter – usually a bolthole as quickly as possible.

While the clan is out foraging, they constantly communicate with one another by softly growling. This continuous communication helps them keep track of each other's location. Juvenile meerkats tend to make a louder noise while foraging, which can be heard up to 90 meters away. In the event that they become separated from the rest of the clan their call increases in volume enabling the elders to locate the lost member.

Body language forms another important part of suricate communication and in particular the position of their tail.

■ ABOVE: **Minders with the young on alert, Botswana.**

■ OPPOSITE: **On guard, looking to the skies for potential predators.**

■ ABOVE: **A pack taking time to do some much needed grooming.**

Meerkats have long slender tails with dark tips, which they hold up in the air while foraging for food; this is another means for identification within the clan and can help clan members locate one another.

Much like many other animals, the position of a meerkat's tail can give an indication of the mood that they are in. As a general rule, when the tail is down they are calm and submissive. When they hold it erect in the air it is a sign that they are alert and responsive. This is evident in behavior such as play fighting, mobbing, and when in combat. Scent marking is another form of communication and meerkats are able to do this by rubbing their cheeks or by rubbing their scent pouches (under their tails) on rocks and plants.

Meerkats will groom and lick one another, especially around the face. This is so that they all smell alike, as their clan scent is in their saliva. Scent marking is used to determine the clan's territory and is often done by the alpha male of the group.

Meerkats are incredibly social animals that thrive in their co-operative communities. Aside from their daily tasks of foraging, sentry duty, babysitting, and burrow excavation, they also actively participate in and enjoy grooming sessions, playing, wrestling, and, occasionally, racing. Researchers studying them have also been astounded to see them taking part in a "singing ceremony," where the meerkats come together and create a yodeling sound.

Diet and Foraging

■ **ABOVE: Searching for food, Gweta, Makgadikgadi Pans, Botswana.**

■ **BELOW: Eating a scorpion, a succulent meal.**

The diet of a meerkat is varied, and their habitat provides them with a rich source of food to forage for. Surprisingly, they are classed as omnivores as they eat both meat and plant matter but their diet is largely a carnivorous one. They spend the majority of their day searching for food within their territory.

Primarily, meerkats are insectivores and more than 82 per cent of their diet is made up of insects and their larvae. Their sharp teeth are perfectly designed for crunching through exoskeletons, and insects are a particularly good source of nutrition. They reproduce rapidly, meaning that they are usually in good supply providing an almost constant source of food. The types of insects indigenous to the Kalahari include worms, crickets, termites, ants, and beetles, and meerkats will hunt for these and their larvae. Spiders and scorpions make up to seven per cent of the meerkat diet. Spiders are a welcome source of nourishment and meerkats have been seen to feast on baboon spiders (more commonly known as tarantulas) and sun spiders. Many people believe that meerkats are immune to scorpion venom but this is not strictly true. Meerkats have indeed honed their scorpion hunting skills and have developed a resistance to scorpion venom, however if bitten by a particularly deadly species they can still

become ill and may die. The Kalahari Desert is home to the orange-colored parabuthus granulatus (granulated scorpion), one of Africa's most venomous scorpions, and the parabuthus raudus, the largest and most common scorpion found in the region. The meerkat method of catching and killing a scorpion is a skill they develop as pups through lessons with their elders. First, the meerkat will grab the tail and bite off and discard the deadly stinger. With the scorpion "disarmed" the meerkat then drags the body through the sand to remove any further traces of venom from its prey's exoskeleton. The scorpion is then devoured. This method of dragging the prey through the sand is also seen when a meerkat catches a millipede. It was once thought that the meerkats were simply toying with their food but observation and research has led to the conclusion that the meerkats are in fact cleaning the millipedes of the toxins they release to discourage predators.

Lessons in scorpion hunting are taught in stages. Dead scorpions are given to the pups in the first instance. As they get older they are given scorpions with their stingers removed, enabling the young pups to practice dragging their prey through the sand before eating. Finally, they will have the chance to prepare and kill a live scorpion once they have developed the necessary skills to do so.

Meerkats will also eat small lizards, birds, eggs, and small rodents, should such a meal present itself. They also eat plants, roots, and fruit, although this only makes up a very small part of their diet, as vegetation is limited.

Foraging is a daily requirement that takes place in groups. While a sentry keeps a watchful eye for predators in the sky and on the surrounding plains, the rest of the clan will begin searching for food in the undergrowth and in the sand. Although they forage together, they catch and eat their food alone as small regular portions are easier to digest. Depending on the availability of food in the area, meerkats will spread out between six and 45 feet apart. The Kalahari flora is predominantly evergreen thorny scrub including ghaap (hoodia cactus) and the Kalahari Desert melon, an important source of hydration to animals in the area. Common trees found in the Kalahari include the camel thorn and shepherd tree and meerkats will use their muscular hind legs to aid tree climbing for sentry duty. The lush vegetation and long grasses provide the meerkats with a plentiful supply of roots to eat and insects hiding in the undergrowth. During the winter months, when the vegetation is in short supply, the meerkats are forced to spread further afield in search of a meal. Communication is vital and the meerkats regularly call out to one another while they are foraging to ensure that no one gets lost.

■ **OPPOSITE: Foraging while others stand guard in the Kalahari Desert, Botswana.**

■ **BELOW: Success: a meerkat enjoying a lizard for lunch.**

Meerkats have a superb sense of smell and are able to locate insects and grubs underground. Their front claws are curved, and with powerful forearms they are able to shovel sand and dirt out of the way. They often have to move their bodyweight in sand just to find a single insect before moving on to the next spot.

Meerkats have fascinated scientists with their altruistic behavior. An adult meerkat will stay at the burrow on babysitting duty while the mother of the pups will spend the day foraging. It is essential for the lactating female to forage for food in order to get the appropriate amount of nutrition required to produce milk to feed her young. Other adult meerkats will sometimes hunt for the babysitters and the pups that are waiting back at the den.

As the pups begin to venture out of the burrows they practice digging and foraging with their elders. Although they instinctively know how to dig, foraging is a learned skill and during the first few months the pups will beg for their food. They will often follow one of the adults and assist with catching prey.

Adult meerkats will respond to pups with the loudest begging call and will feed them first. As the pups get older the sound of the begging calls change and this no longer provokes the adults to supply them with food. By this time, the pups have become juveniles and are more experienced in foraging for their own meals.

The role of sentry is shared between all adult members of the clan, and this role is on a rotational basis ensuring they all get the opportunity to forage. Meerkats are prey for martial eagles, jackals, and servals so sentry duty is an essential part of a meerkat's daily routine.

Water is scarce in the Kalahari Desert, and meerkats have adapted well to suit the environment. They are able to obtain much of their water requirement from the food that they eat which is why the roots and tubers of plants are an essential part of the meerkat's diet. In addition, the succulent insects they devour provide them with ample hydration.

Anatomy

The adult meerkat has a long slender body that is typically 10-14 inches (25-35 cm) long including the head and limbs (while in a standing position). Its tail is surprisingly long for such a small animal giving an added length of seven-10 inches (17-25 cm). When they are on all four paws, their height is only six inches (15 cm). Meerkats reach full maturity by the age of 12 months, and the average male meerkat weighs in at approximately 2.1 lbs (952g) while females are typically slightly lighter, weighing in at approximately 1.6 lbs (725g).

Although the meerkat is a small mammal belonging to the herpestid family, it has some distinguishable differences to its mongoose relations. The first notable difference is that unlike the nocturnal behavior seen in many of the other mongoose species, meerkats are in fact diurnal, only leaving the safety of their burrows in daylight. Another considerable difference is that meerkats live in large communities while other species of Herpestidae prefer a more solitary lifestyle, either living alone or in pairs. There are only three other species of mongoose that share the meerkats' social groups: the banded mongoose, the common kusimanse, and the common dwarf mongoose. Interestingly, these species also share the meerkats' diurnal behavior. There are also some key differences when looking deeper at the meerkat appearance and anatomy.

Meerkats have small, dark-colored crescent-shaped ears that are set low on each side of the head. Their unique feature is that the ears are in fact closeable, which keeps out sand and dirt when they are digging. Their ears are remarkably receptive however and are still able to pick up an alarm call while "closed."

Unlike other members of the herpestid family, the meerkat does not have a bushy tail; instead it has a thin tapered tail. Measuring between seven and 10 inches long, the tail almost matches the length of the meerkat's body. The tail has multiple uses and is a great asset to the meerkat as they often use their long tails for balance when standing on their hind legs, creating a tripod effect. The tail is often brown in color with a black or darker tip. During snake mobbing, the meerkat uses their tail to confuse the snake, causing it to strike the tail opposed to the head, saving the meerkat from what could be a fatal bite. The meerkat tail is also an important part of their body language and is an additional tool for communication. When held up high and straight the animal is excited or alarmed, and when down the meerkat is calm and submissive in behavior.

Both male and female meerkats have short hair. The color of their coat varies between subspecies and has much to do with their habitat, giving the meerkats camouflage. Typical colors include fawn, tan, gray, and various shades of brown. Meerkats found in the Namib Desert tend to have light tan

■ **ABOVE: On guard duty, Kgalagadi Transfrontier Park, South Africa.**

■ **LEFT:** **Sharp teeth prove useful when dealing with prey.**

■ **OPPOSITE:** **Using long tails to balance, Kgalagadi Transfrontier Park, South Africa.**

■ **BELOW:** **Meerkats have four non-retractable claws on each paw.**

coats, while those in the Kalahari Desert have adapted to the brighter terrain and typically have light brown or orange coats. The species that live in the green scrublands of South Africa have coats that are dark brown in color.

Each meerkat has a set of unique stripes across their back between the base of the tail and the shoulders and no two meerkats share the same markings. The underside of the animal has no markings and has only a thin layer of hair revealing a patch of dark skin. This patch acts like a built-in solar panel, conducting heat in order to provide warmth after cool nights in the desert. Their fur has the superb ability to keep meerkats well insulated through cold nights, as well as to prevent them from overheating during hot days.

All meerkats, regardless of their subspecies, have the distinct dark rings around their eyes which assist in reducing glare from the sun, allowing them to stare out across the desert and bright sky. Meerkats have exceptional eyesight enabling them to spot a predator up to three quarters of a mile away. As farsighted mammals, their ability to see things up close is not as good and they often rely on their sense of smell to find food when it's right in front of them. The eyes have a nictitating membrane between the eye and the eyelid that removes any caught sand with every blink. This is particularly useful when they are digging and foraging for food. They have a wide range of vision thanks to long horizontal pupils.

Meerkat faces and throats are predominantly a shade of white, with their faces tapering to a snout. Pups are born with pink noses and stay pink if they are female. The noses of males turn completely black as they age. Meerkats have an excellent sense of smell, which they use to identify other members of the clan, locate prey, and sniff out rival meerkats. Their noses are highly receptive to scent and from it they are able to judge how recent a rival meerkat has been in the area and from which group they came from. Scent marking is considered to be of great importance to meerkats, as they use smell to mark out territory and identify family members. They have scent glands on their cheeks and in the anal region and both serve an important purpose. Cheek marking, using saliva, is reserved for members of the clan whereas anal marking is used for marking out and claiming territory.

Meerkats have extremely sharp teeth, designed for breaking through the tough exoskeletons of prey items. They have between 36 and 40 teeth including four canines, 12 incisors, at least 12 premolars, and between four and eight molars. Their fangs are the ideal tools for catching and killing prey. Their fangs are also used in combat with rival meerkats where they are used to latch on to their opponent. This technique can even be used against predators, although it is a rare occurrence.

The meerkat's claws are non-retractable and can reach lengths of up to two cm (0.8 inches) on average. With four claws on each paw (totaling 16) this gives the meerkat a great advantage when needing to dig or burrow in the presence of a predator. With a combination of their powerful forearms and curved claws they can shift an amount of sand equal to their own bodyweight in a matter of seconds. When engaged in combat, meerkats have been known to use their claws as a means of striking their opponents, however they usually favor using their fangs instead. The meerkat also uses its claws to forage for food and to climb bushes, logs, and trees when scouting for danger. Another use for their sharp claws is to dig and shape their extensive complex underground burrows.

Meerkats have strong muscular hind legs that enable them to stand up (with assistance from the tail). They have thick padded feet that not only aid the meerkat's need to stand, but also allow them to sprint across terrain at a speed of up to 20mph (32kmph).

Reproduction and Young

Meerkats are unique creatures in terms of their reproductive behavior. Breeding is usually reserved for the dominant pair, although subordinates that become pregnant can be a cause for change within the group.

Females become sexually active from the age of 10 months and are temporarily forced out of the clan, along with any other subordinate females, by the alpha female when she is getting ready to breed. Once she has given birth to her pups, and has regained her strength, she will allow the briefly evicted females back into the group. This behavior has several purposes. First, it raises stress levels in the evicted females, which reduces hormone levels so that they have a lower chance of becoming pregnant themselves. Studies have shown that the stress levels can peak to the point that they become infertile. If any of the beta females happen to be pregnant when they are evicted from the clan, the stress levels usually end up being the cause of them aborting their pups. Only a few subordinates do end up giving birth to live young, and those that do try to sneak them back into the clan. The alpha female is an aggressive leader, however, and will kill and eat the beta female's pups. The chances of the pups being accepted as part of the clan are very slim.

Second, the alpha female is vulnerable when she has just given birth and a subordinate female may use this opportunity to overthrow her and assert her dominance within the clan. Third, the alpha female wants the very best start in life for her offspring and will let the subordinates back into the clan once the pups are a few days old. Many beta females allo-lactate and will feed the pups while the dominant female forages for food.

■ **ABOVE: A mother and her newborn pups.**

■ **BELOW: A meerkat adult gives its pup a lift.**

Meerkats are able to reproduce all year round, and can breed every two months if they choose to. They usually successfully breed two to three times a year and tend to do this between October and April when there is an abundance of food. The alpha female must accept the alpha male for reproduction to commence. The male will persistently groom and stroke the female to encourage her to yield, a courtship ritual that can last for hours. The male will then bite the back of her neck and latch on to the female so that mating can take

■ **ABOVE: Meerkat babies venturing out, Kalahari Desert, South Africa.**

■ ABOVE: **Young meerkats learning through play.**

place. The gestational period is approximately 70 days (10 weeks). The pregnant female will gain as much as 40 per cent of her body weight throughout this time.

She gives birth to the pups during the night down in the breeding burrow and typical litters are made up of three to five pups. They are born with their eyes closed and have only a thin covering of fur. The first few days of the pups lives are their most challenging, as infanticide is high from pregnant females that want to increase the survival rates of their own pups. Studies have shown that the risk of infanticide significantly reduces after four days. If the alpha female senses that a subordinate is pregnant, she will evict her to protect the lives of her own pups. Sometimes evicted females are allowed back in the clan once they have had their pups, but on many occasions they will rove in the hope that they can find a new group to join.

For the first fortnight, the newborn pups remain in the cozy sleeping burrow and will suckle milk from their mother and

allo-lactating females in the clan. Lactation in beta females is more common in those that have recently aborted a litter, as the hormone oxytocin is high. This hormone is also largely responsible for the allo-parental behavior seen in rearing young. The higher levels of oxytocin leads to them spending more time with the pups and spending less time foraging. The pups will open their eyes for the first time when they are 10 days old, and will open their ears between 10 and 14 days old.

When the pups are around three weeks old they will start to emerge from their underground burrow under the supervision of the babysitters. They weigh only 100g and will stay close to the burrow under the watchful eye of their babysitters. It is at this time that they will usually move to a new den as the parasitic burden becomes too high. Moving to a new den also allows the insect numbers to multiply after the clan has exhausted it. The alpha female is not required to take part in sentry duty and will spend much of her time foraging in order to help replenish her milk supply and strength.

Between the age of four and six months the pups will follow their elders and mimic foraging. At this age they are still getting nutrition from milk and will supplement their diet with insects. Between six and 16 weeks of age they will start foraging for their own food, as they will no longer be receiving milk. Pups of this age still have a lot to learn and usually receive much of their food through begging from elders. Research has shown that pups that make the loudest begging call will get the most food. By the time they are three months old, they are classed as juveniles and will have to forage for much of their own food. Hormonal and developmental changes in the young meerkats mean that adults no longer respond to their begging calls.

Many of the survival and foraging skills are learned rather than instinctual. The juveniles are mentored by older and more experienced members of the clan. They learn how to handle and kill prey, which is a particularly important skill when handling venomous creatures such as scorpions. They are first given dead prey to play with before being given a live scorpion with the deadly stinger removed. Once they handle these prey items confidently they are given opportunities to immobilize and kill their own prey items.

Communication is another vital skill that the juveniles must develop, as they need to know how to signal or respond to a warning call. Meerkats of all ages will play fight among one another and this behavior helps teach the juveniles fighting techniques. These skills come in useful during a meerkat's lifetime as they use them to assert dominance, fight a meerkat from a rival gang, and will also use them for mobbing purposes.

Meerkats reach adulthood at the age of 12 months, although they can be sexually active from around 10 months. It is unlikely that a female of this age would have a litter of her own. Usually, females have their first successful litter at around the age of two years old if they have become the dominant leader within a group. Yearling meerkats play a more active role within their clan and will take part in babysitting and sentry duties.

After reaching maturity many males leave their birth clan in order to search for better breeding opportunities and in the hope that they can become the dominant male of a group and have pups of their own.

■ **OPPOSITE: A young meerkat being looked after in the Kalahari Desert, South Africa.**

■ **RIGHT: Warming in the sun, young meerkats learn what to do from their elders.**

Behavior

■ ABOVE: **On sentry duty, Makgadikgadi Pans, Kalahari Desert, Botswana.**
■ BELOW: **Hierarchy is important. Here, meerkats show their aggression.**

Meerkats live in co-operative societies. The behavior that they display has long been a point of interest to behavioral scientists and studies have been carried out to better understand the complex social structure of clans. It is this sophisticated social structure that enables them to thrive in the harsh desert conditions. It was first thought that each meerkat had a well-defined role within the clan, but through recent studies and careful observation it has been discovered that this is not the case. Research suggests that hormonal changes influence their behavior and that meerkats display genuine altruistic tendencies through sentry duty and babysitting pups.

The characteristics of their behavior suggest that they are one of the most complex species of animal on earth. The social structure begins with dominance and meerkats live in a matriarchal community, which means that females have complete power over the group.

Alpha Female

The alpha female is the dominant female in the group, and reserves all breeding rights, and for this reason, is usually the mother of all the pups in the clan. They act upon this exclusivity by killing any pups born to subordinate females. As the leader of the group, the dominant female gets to choose her partner. If the dominant male of the group does not get accepted he is evicted from the clan. The alpha female leads the group out for foraging, will determine which sleeping burrows to use, and when to move to a new den.

Females born into the clan always fall into the subordinate role and

remain submissive to the alpha female. As they grow older they start to challenge one another in order to grow in status and display dominance; typical behavior includes growling, fighting, hip slamming, and stealing food. Once a subordinate has dominated all other females of the same rank she will challenge the alpha female. Meerkats are vicious fighters and the heaviest and strongest female wins the fight for leadership. If the alpha female is beaten by a subordinate, she is usually attacked until she is evicted from the group, regardless of whether she is the sister or mother of the newly appointed alpha. The new dominant female has to assert her dominance constantly and usually there is little fuss from other members of the clan. Studies have shown that newly dominant females have increased levels of estradiol and cortisol, which makes them more aggressive and extremely hierarchical. Research has proven that hormone levels correlate with age and body weight. The dominant female will start to breed and reproduce young of her own as soon as she has accepted a male partner.

On average, the alpha female will be the dominant leader for approximately 31 months before being challenged by a subordinate. If the dominant female dies, subordinates begin to challenge one another in the hope that they become the new alpha female of the group. Usually it is the eldest

■ ABOVE LEFT: **A close-up of a meerkat sticking its head outside the burrow, Gweta, Makgadikgadi Pans, Botswana.**

■ ABOVE RIGHT: **Meerkats showing more aggression.**

that claims the title but occasionally it is the most aggressive individual that wins the role of authority. As previously stated, the exclusivity of breeding is reserved for the alpha female and she will attack subordinates to assert dominance. This behavior also lowers estrogen levels in the beta females, reducing their chances of becoming pregnant. Pregnancy also triggers aggression among the female members of the clan. Pregnant beta females are often no longer submissive to the alpha female, which leads to dominance fights. This results in the subordinate being permanently evicted from the clan or the dominant female being overthrown.

Alpha Male

The alpha male is the dominant male of the clan and, although he is not as powerful as the alpha female, he still displays his power through aggression toward other males. Their role includes marking the territory of the clan around the burrow and scouting to mark the outer boundaries of the territory.

Similarly to the maturing females, male meerkats begin to show their dominance within the group as they grow in size and age. They instinctively start to challenge the dominant male, regardless of whether he is a father or brother. However, unlike the females, the former dominant male is not always evicted from the group, although he may be subjected to bullying from the new alpha male.

If the alpha female dies, the dominant male will leave the group in order to seek new mating opportunities, as most of the females within the group are his offspring. Interestingly, male meerkats are able to identify their own offspring and will not mate with them. Similarly, female meerkats know who their brothers are, even if they are separated as juveniles and grow up in different groups. In these instances, the females always refuse their brothers' mating attempts.

If the dominant male leaves the clan, the beta males will fight aggressively to become the new alpha of the group.

Roving Meerkats

Unlike many females, males tend to start off in other clans. Male meerkats are forced to leave their birth clan between the ages of one and two years old in order to seek mating opportunities, as they are usually related to all the females within their clan.

Meerkats that have left a group are called rovers and usually seek a new clan either alone or in pairs. Occasionally a group of roving males will join a new clan and will overthrow the current alpha male, as they are unrelated to the females of the group they are potential mates for the alpha female. Female roving is rare, and is usually done because of eviction from a clan rather than by choice. Joining an established group is very rare for females and they often stand a better chance of joining a newly formed group.

Meerkats depend on their co-operative social structure to survive. A single meerkat can survive for up to a year if there is sufficient food and a predator does not attack them.

Beta Males and Females

The subordinate meerkats within the clan support the alpha male and female. Their duties include babysitting and helping raise the pups, many of which are their brothers and sisters, and this duty is shared between males and females.

Many beta males and females choose to leave the clan before they are three years old, in order to search for better breeding opportunities.

Beta females are temporarily driven from their clan while the alpha female is getting ready to breed. The escalating aggression and short-term eviction causes the subordinates to become highly stressed, reducing their likelihood of being able to successfully breed. Studies have even shown that this behavior can cause infertility within the subordinates and can also lead to abortion if any of the beta females are already pregnant. The constant aggression shown from the alpha female causes the subordinates to suppress reproduction, which enables the pups born to the dominant female to have the very best start in life as there is no competition for food or care.

Meerkat Roles Within the Clan

In addition to babysitting and sentry duty, meerkats will also work together to excavate and maintain their burrows, mentor pups, take part in daily grooming, and play fighting. Both males and females within the clan perform all of these duties.

Babysitters are subordinates over six months old that stay at the burrows to care for the pups while the rest of the clan forage for food. Those that stay behind to help rear young often sacrifice their opportunity to forage, although occasionally other members of the clan will bring food back to the burrows for them.

Babysitters also have to protect the vulnerable young from danger even at the risk of their own life. If they are unable to take the pups down to the safety of the burrow they will gather them together and lie on top of them.

Sentry duty is a vital part of meerkat society. As the clan forages for food, the sentry will vigilantly watch the sky and vast savannah for danger. Meerkats are agile climbers and will climb a tree up to 30 feet in order to get the best vantage point. A sentry will also keep watch at the burrow and this is done from the ground or by climbing a bush or tree. If danger is present, the sentinel will alert the rest of the clan with a unique barking signal.

Grooming is a daily part of meerkat life. Not only do they remove parasites from one another, the natural reflex of grooming strengthens social bonds. Meerkats are often hosts to fleas and ticks so grooming is a welcome activity within the clan. They will actually eat the parasites, although they do not form part of the usual diet. Grooming also lowers the heart rate and encourages relaxation. This stress-reducing activity is thought to be an important part of their close-knit community.

When a rival gang or roving meerkats invade a clan's territory, the group bunch together, puff up their coats, and will jump up and down making a lot of noise. This intimidating behavior is called mobbing and is frequently seen in avian species as well as some other animals. Occasionally it will deter the intruders but often it will lead to a fight. Meerkats are aggressive fighters and are highly territorial: they will kill rivals if they can.

Mobbing behavior is also used against a predator that threatens the group. Meerkats have been seen to form an intimidating circle around a snake, closing in around the predator with spit calls.

Adult meerkats between the age of one and two years have been seen to mob a snake more persistently than a juvenile or older meerkat and it is thought that this is part of the social learning and hormonal changes that they go through.

■ **ABOVE: Meerkats play fighting, Kgalagadi Transfrontier Park, South Africa.**

■ **LEFT: Meerkats grooming each other.**

Population

■ **ABOVE: A meerkat family standing guard, Makgadikgadi Pans, Kalahari Desert, Botswana.**

Meerkats have a "least concern" conservation status and are not at risk of becoming endangered. It is believed that there are approximately 500,000 meerkats living wild in the southern Africa regions of Kalahari, Botswana, and Namibia. Considering that wild meerkats are exclusive to this area of the world, this vast number of meerkats could be considered quite a dense population considering the small area of inhabitance.

With families that include relatives sticking together in burrows and the strict breeding that meerkats follow, this keeps the population steady and at a very low risk of potential extinction. The meerkat breeding code is strict and therefore limits the amount of newborns within a given community. Most commonly a meerkat clan features around 20 suricates, however bigger families do exist and can consist of 50 family members or more.

The average lifespan is approximately 10 years in the wild, although many pups don't make it beyond their first year, and those that do not become dominant as they grow up rarely make it past the age of three.

It is only the dominant female that has the exclusive breeding rights in each meerkat community, which could be considered a basic form of population control. Only the strongest members of the clan are able to pass on their genes to offspring. Alongside this, another contributing factor of the meerkat community size is the availability or scarceness of food and the varying predator types that hunt in the different territorial regions. It is likely that where there is more food, the family sizes will be larger.

Long-term Survival

■ **ABOVE:** **A thunder and lightning storm over the Kalahari, Khutse Game Reserve, Botswana.**

The long-term survival of meerkats has several contributing factors. Although they are classed as "least concern" by the IUCN, they are threatened by various factors including climate, predators, diseases, and habitat loss from human encroachment. During the summer months, the Kalahari region is transformed from a dry dusty terrain to a lush green environment thanks to the rain of the wet season. Although the abundance of vegetation and rise of prey increases during this season, with it comes a potential threat of flooding to the meerkat clan and their newborn pups. When the rain approaches, the sentry will use an alarm call to alert the others. Rainfall is unpredictable in the Kalahari Desert and thunderstorms can be sudden and heavy, increasing the risk of flooding in the burrows. Once the sentry has raised the alarm, the alpha female will carry the young pups on her back to higher ground. Unfortunately, if a sudden downpour occurs during the night, the clan has no warning and may become trapped in the flooding burrow system.

The Kalahari Desert supports many species, which is particularly useful to meerkats when they are foraging for prey items. Unfortunately this also means that meerkats themselves are potential prey to many predatory creatures in the region and a large number of meerkats are killed defending the clan's pups. Living in large groups, having a sentry on duty, and access to burrows and boltholes are a necessity for these small mammals, and this gives them some security. Aerial predators are the biggest threat to meerkats, with the Kalahari Desert being home to martial eagles, bateleurs, and giant eagle owls.

Snakes, such as the cape cobra, puff adder, and mole snakes, pose a threat to meerkats, especially when there are pups in the burrow, so mobbing discourages the predator from invading a meerkat's territory. There are also a number of terrestrial predators, including black-backed jackals, cape foxes, servals, and genets.

Meerkat predator profiles:

Black-backed jackal

The black-backed jackal is a foxlike omnivore that weighs between 15 and 30 lbs. They have a distinctive reddish coat color with a black and gray back and tail. They are opportunistic eaters and will feed on a varied diet, ranging from invertebrates to small mammals such as hares, mongooses, and rodents. They tend to hunt in packs in the evening.

Cape fox

Sometimes known as the silver-backed fox, this predator weighs around 11 lbs and hunts small mammals and invertebrates, although it will not turn down a meal in the form of a reptile or bird should the opportunity arise. These nocturnal hunters give the meerkats good reason to stay in their burrows at night, as they will prey on the pups given the chance.

Serval

Referred to as "the little cats of Africa," these feline predators can jump as high as 10 feet in the air and can reach a top running speed of 50mph. They are extremely intelligent, with acute hearing that can detect underground burrowers. They have black spots on golden fur and have distinctive facial features, including large ears.

Genet

These Feliforms are related to cats but share a closer relationship with mongooses. They have silver-grey coats with black spots and long banded tails. They are agile climbers and will spend much of their time in a tree and will hunt at sunrise and sunset, although juvenile genets are active during the day. Although they are classed as omnivores they prefer a more carnivorous diet and tend to eat a diet consisting of small rodents, shrews, and bats; given the opportunity they would welcome a meerkat pup as a meal.

Cape cobra

This highly venomous snake is a diurnal predator that is common in the Kalahari Desert and feeds on rodents, lizards, and birds. The cape cobra is regarded as one of the most dangerous snakes in Africa. They often inhabit former rodent burrows but given the chance will prey on meerkat pups. By contrast, meerkats are ironically known to be predatory animals to the cape cobra due to their mobbing tactics.

- **TOP:** **Cape foxes on the lookout for prey.**
- **ABOVE:** **The serval in majestic full flow.**
- **OPPOSITE:** **A black-backed jackal.**
- **BELOW:** **The small-spotted Genet.**

■ ABOVE: The venomous cape cobra.

Puff adder

Approximately a meter in length, the puff adder is another threat to meerkats in southern Africa. They are able to strike rapidly and return to a tightly coiled defensive position if provoked. They have long, highly venomous fangs that easily penetrate their prey's flesh.

Mole snake

Mole snakes often live in abandoned burrows and can pose a threat to meerkat pups. They can grow up to two meters in length. Mole snakes are very common in the Kalahari region and although they are not venomous they do have an aggressive nature and can cause severe bite wounds.

Martial eagle

These aerial hunters are the meerkats' most feared predator. With a wingspan of six feet they are the largest of the eagle species found in Africa. They have excellent eyesight and are able to spot prey up to three and a half miles away. Their hunting tactic is to circle high above their potential prey before swooping down suddenly at high speeds using the element of surprise to capture their next victim. A meerkat sentry will raise an urgent alarm the moment they spot a martial eagle in their territory. They are so fearful of aerial predators that even a light aircraft will send them scurrying back to the safety of their burrows.

Bateleur eagle

The bateleur is a type of eagle that is found in various places, including South Africa. It is a colorful species that has a wingspan of up to six feet and can spend up to nine hours per day in the air searching for food. Although they prefer to prey on small birds, they will hunt rodents and other small mammals, making meerkats a favorable target.

Predators aren't the only threat to suricates. They are often at risk from rival clans intruding on marked territory, newly formed groups looking to claim a territory, or a group of roving males looking for breeding opportunities in another clan. Meerkats will fiercely defend their territory and will fight if it is necessary. As a species, meerkats are susceptible to diseases, such as bovine tuberculosis, and are also significant carriers of rabies.

Humans pose a threat to meerkats in the wild as they contribute to habitat loss and fatalities on the road. Unfortunately, many people also want to keep meerkats as pets, which they are not suited for due to the complex social structure and behavior they strongly depend upon. It is illegal to keep a meerkat as a pet in the United States.

■ ABOVE: Another venomous snake, the puff adder.

■ LEFT: The martial eagle, a fearsome predator for meerkat populations.

■ RIGHT: A bateleur eagle about to land.

■ OVERLEAF: Keeping an eye on a 4x4 vehicle as it drives through the grasslands of the Makgadikgadi, Botswana.

Conservation and Popular Culture

■ **ABOVE: A meerkat tentatively leaving the burrow, Kalahari Desert, Botswana.**

The suricate species are not likely to become endangered in the near future. However, they are a vital part of the ecosystem in the Kalahari Desert and Namib Desert, and efforts are being made to conserve the species in their natural environment. The Kalahari Meerkat Project is a long-term research project that contributes to the study of these fascinating creatures and the evolution of co-operative behavior. The project was founded in 1993 at the Kuruman River Reserve by professor Tim Clutton-Brock and is co-operatively owned by the University of Cambridge and the Kalahari Research Trust. They have worked closely with the producers of various meerkat-focused documentaries.

In 1989, Fellow Earthlings Wildlife Center was founded in California. The non-profit organization specializes in caring for meerkats that are injured, orphaned, old, or sick. While they are not specifically conserving meerkats in their native environment, the center partnered with Animal Planet for *Meerkat Manor* and played a part in National Geographic's documentary film *Meerkat Madness*; it continues to raise awareness of the species.

Meerkats became popular culture celebrities with the rise of *Meerkat Manor*, and before that Disney's animated classic *The Lion King*, but these fascinating creatures captured the hearts of mankind in the 1980s when the first wildlife documentaries featuring these social creatures were first aired. In the United Kingdom, in 1987, Sir David Attenborough's documentary *Meerkats United* was aired as part of the *Wildlife on One* series, and for the first time people were able to visually engage with the intriguing and captivating study of the suricate species. The documentary focused on the habitual attributes and the social hierarchy of meerkat clans. *Meerkats United* became one of the BBC's most popular broadcast shows and was aired worldwide due to popular demand.

■ **ABOVE:** **British television wildlife documentary maker, Sir David Attenborough.**

■ **OPPOSITE:** **Timon attends a *Lion King* premier in Rome.**

■ **OVERLEAF:** ***Meerkat Manor*** **proved to be an enormous worldwide success, with its unique look at meerkat families.**

In 1994, one particular fictional animated meerkat made it to box offices and theaters worldwide when Walt Disney Pictures released *The Lion King*. *The Lion King*, a story based in Africa that covers moral views of family, territory, and sacrifice, saw a meerkat star created in the form of the character known as Timon (voiced by Nathan Lane). Timon was a cheeky and disorganized character that often claimed others' ideas as his own. Timon is a name associated with Greek history, that translates to "he who respects," which could be considered to be quite fitting with the meerkat habitual tendencies that have been studied. The success of the animated picture really put a mark on the worldwide recognition of meerkats. Later, a spin-off children's television series of *Timon & Pumbaa* was aired in the US between 1995 and 1998.

In 2005, Oxford Scientific Films produced a television show for Animal Planet that would capture the hearts of the nation. In September of that year, *Meerkat Manor* premiered after it was well received in the United Kingdom. *Meerkat Manor* soon became an international success and continued for three further seasons until the show was canceled in August 2009. The success of the show was a combination of dramatic narration over a typical wildlife documentary style format, which focused on a family of meerkats called the Whiskers clan. By working closely with the Kalahari Meerkat Project, the producers of the show were able to show viewers never before seen footage of the suricates' complex social hierarchy, and behavior through experimental and innovative filming techniques. The Whiskers family became the stars of the show, with the audience captivated by both the heartwarming and tragic events shown.

Overall, *Meerkat Manor* was a success although it faced criticism for not intervening when a meerkat was suffering from an injury. When the show's alpha female (Flower) was bitten by a snake and subsequently died, many viewers became upset and wrote in to complain that more should have been done to save her. The producers issued a statement to clarify the policy of intervention. As the research facility monitors the breeding success and survival of individuals, intervening would have made the investigation valueless.

Meerkat Manor went on to be nominated for two Primetime Emmy Awards, and won awards at the Omni Awards and the New York Festival Award Gala. Following its success, the television film *Meerkat Manor: The Story Begins* was aired in May 2008, which documented Flower's birth and rise to alpha female of the clan. Since the success of *Meerkat Manor*, several other movies and documentaries have made it to the screen. The Kalahari Meerkat Project has contributed to a number of these productions including:

DEL FILM DI ROMA
BNL

Meerkat Madness (2000), *Meerkats* (2003), and *Ella, a Meerkat's Tale* (2005).

Over in the UK, in January 2009, meerkats became a fascination amongst the nation's residents after a comparative car insurance website (owned by BGL Group) used them in a four-year-long advertising campaign to market their services. A clever take on the advertising campaign was to ensure that members of the public were to check the spelling of the website address when searching the web for "comparethemarket.com," as apparently many people were misspelling the website address and instead inputting "comparethemeerkat.com." What started as a simple humorous idea for selling car insurance, soon led to an outburst for the market need for everything meerkat. Soon after the advertisement first aired in the UK, local novelty shops began to stock meerkat merchandise, from t-shirts to garden statues, and plush toys to undergarments.

The creators/founders of comparethemarket.com came up with the ingenious idea of using two specific meerkat characters to bring the species' tales of woe and strife to life: Aleksandr Orlov (a successful Russian "businesskat") and Sergei (the I.T. technician). The television advertisements featured the two characters and small visual snippets of their previous feats, always finishing with the lead character (Aleksandr) shouting "It's comparethemarket.com, not comparethemeerkat.com… simples!" Some of this quote was used in many satirical British comedies, such as *The Inbetweeners*.

The sudden fascination with meerkats in the UK, led to the BBC releasing meerkat wildlife specials and an endless range of novelty merchandise being manufactured on a massive scale; Aleksandr even released an autobiography in 2010 titled *A Simples Life: The Life and Times of Aleksandr Orlov*. The effectiveness of the marketing campaign was easy to measure. Due to popular demand, the insurance company started manufacturing their own official plush toy characters, as an incentive for more people to insure through them. The idea being that when you buy insurance from comparethemarket.com, you get a free toy character each time you renew. Later, the same television advertisements and campaign aired in Australia, pushing the meerkat madness further worldwide.

■ **ABOVE: An Aleksandr Orlov meerkat "talking toy," in the meerkat enclosure at London Zoo, sold exclusively in Harrods, London.**

■ **OPPOSITE: Meerkats have provided much amusement and inspiration for the media.**

Useful Websites

www.kalahari-meerkats.com

http://friends.kalahari-meerkats.com/

http://www.fellowearthlings.org/info.html

http://animals.sandiegozoo.org/animals/meerkat

http://www.lazoo.org/animals/mammals/meerkat/

http://animals.nationalgeographic.co.uk/animals/mammals/meerkat/

http://science.howstuffworks.com/zoology/mammals/meerkats1.htm

http://www.nhm.ac.uk/nature-online/species-of-the-day/common-species/suricata-suricatta/index.html

http://www.cam.ac.uk/research/news/research-suggests-meerkat-predator-scanning-behaviour-is-altruistic

http://animal.discovery.com/mammals/meerkat-dominant-female.htm

http://www.meerkatmanor.co.uk/

http://www.livescience.com/27406-meerkats.html